A BOOK OF PASTORAL PRAYERS

A Book of Pastoral Prayers

WITH AN ESSAY ON

The Pastoral Prayer

By

ERNEST FREMONT TITTLE

NEW YORK NASHVILLE

 ABINGDON-COKESBURY PRESS

A BOOK OF PASTORAL PRAYERS

COPYRIGHT MCMLI BY PIERCE AND SMITH

The essay "The Pastoral Prayer" is reprinted from *Religion in Life,* Summer, 1946 Copyright 1946 by Stone and Pierce

SET UP, PRINTED, AND BOUND BY THE PARTHENON PRESS, AT NASHVILLE, TENNESSEE, UNITED STATES OF AMERICA

FOREWORD

By GEORGIA HARKNESS

The author of this book needs no introduction: At the time of his death in August, 1949, he was universally acknowledged to be one of the great preachers of America, a man with whom some might disagree but whom none could do other than respect and admire for his forthright proclamation of the Christian gospel.

Dr. Tittle is known throughout the Church for his prophetic, incisive, clear-thinking sermons. What is perhaps not so well known is that he himself considered the pulpit prayer to be equally if not more important. "It is even arguable that the prayer may be of greater value than the sermon." He expressed this conviction more than once as I sought his wise and honest counsel on the composition of my own prayers.

Current practice calls generally for careful sermon preparation, but often shies away from previous preparation of the pulpit prayer for fear it may be forced and unnatural. So indeed it may be unless it comes from the depths of a soul responsive to the voice and will of God. Such a soul was Ernest Tittle's. He preached great sermons because they came out of hard work and a great, though unobtrusive, life of prayer. He uttered prayers on Sunday morning that could move his

5

congregation to new depths of spirit, lift them to new heights of comfort and challenge, and mediate to them the grace of God because he paid what it cost. This cost was of a twofold nature—personal Christian living and time-consuming, painstaking preparation.

It should be made clear that Dr. Tittle did not read his prayers, or his sermons, on Sunday morning. He prepared them so carefully that they became a part of him and could be spoken from his heart without manuscript. Because he did this work so carefully, it is now possible in this book to garner the fruit of his effort. In response to many requests to publish a volume of prayers he had made the selection before his death, and they are here made available as he left them.

This book will be of incalculable value to all who wish to hear the voice of God through great praying. It will naturally have a special appeal to ministers who have pulpit prayers to make. It is not suggested that they simply read these on Sunday morning. What is more needful is to let the spirit of these prayers and their clear, simple, strong diction saturate one's mind and soul, and then by following the suggestions in Dr. Tittle's article on the pastoral prayer to "go and do likewise." The best tribute to his memory would be through a deepening of skills in this difficult but all-important art to give more comely praise to God.

CONTENTS

The Pastoral Prayer

THE PASTORAL prayer, in all too many cases, is the most neglected part of the service. Hymn, anthem, scripture, sermon all bespeak some measure of premeditation; but the pastoral prayer is "extemporary" in the exact sense that it is uttered on the spur of the moment without previous preparation, mental or spiritual—with the result that it tends to be verbose, slipshod, and ineffective. After the first few words the people grow inattentive, or consciously pained and bored.

Such neglect is something more than a pity; it is a disgrace. When the moment comes to say, "Let us pray," the minister has the opportunity of helping the people to "draw boldly unto the throne of grace, that [they] may receive mercy and find grace to help [them] in time of need." And what greater opportunity does the minister have during the entire course of the service? It is even arguable that the prayer may be of greater value than the sermon. This is not said in depreciation of preaching. The minister may devoutly hope that the sermon, inadequate though it be, will be used of God to set forth his truth and righteousness and redeeming grace—even to turn someone from his sinful wanderings to the way of life. But the possibility remains that the prayer more effectively than the sermon may serve as the medium of a divine approach to the congregation. That this is indeed the case many a minister has been given reason to suppose. Often he has heard words of appreciation for the sermon, followed by the grateful confession, "I was especially helped by the prayer." To neglect the pastoral prayer is to be guilty of a serious sin of omission.

The minister in the nonliturgical church may sometimes wish he were free to dispense with "free" prayer in favor of a liturgical order. The disciplines required for the preparation and delivery of sermons are persistent and exacting enough; but they are hardly to be compared to the disciplines called for by the pastoral prayer, whose purpose is to present before God the unspoken supplications of the people, whose language (ideally) is the language of poetry, and whose helpfulness cannot but be affected by the known character of the ministrant. To meet fully the demands of the pastoral prayer the minister would need to be at once priest, poet, and saint.

The extreme difficulty of extemporary prayer raises the old issue between liturgical and nonliturgical orders of worship. But it may well be the case that public worship should include both formal prayer and free prayer.

The reality and worth of formal prayer has in principle been conceded by any nonliturgical church which administers the Sacrament of Baptism or the Sacrament of the Lord's Supper, or which uses the Lord's Prayer. And, indeed, it must be the case that a prayer read from a book may be quite as real as a prayer spontaneously uttered. To deny this is to hold that the Spirit which prompts to prayer cannot work through words with which the worshiper is familiar but only through words which he is hearing (or speaking) for the first time. And if you take that position when it comes to prayer, what is your position on the use of scripture in public worship? Are you prepared to believe that the Holy Spirit cannot work through the familiar words of the Beatitudes or of the Twenty-third Psalm? Even in free prayer the same ideas and phrases may occur over and over again. Indeed, the pastoral prayer in the nonliturgical church may become as set in its way as any traditional collect, with the difference that, whereas the collect often rises to the level of true religion and great art, the pastoral prayer all too often leaves much to be desired in both diction and thought.

That a read prayer can be a means of grace has been demonstrated in human experience down the ages, and is now being demonstrated in numbers of individual churches of the nonliturgical type where frequent or weekly use is made of the General Thanksgiving:

Almighty God, Father of all mercies, we thine unworthy servants do give thee most humble and hearty thanks for all thy goodness and lovingkindness to us, and to all men. We bless thee for our creation, preservation, and all the blessings of this life; but above all for thine inestimable love in the redemption of the world by our Lord Jesus Christ, for the means of grace, and for the hope of glory. And we beseech thee, give us that due sense of all thy mercies, that our hearts may be unfeignedly thankful, and that we may show forth thy praise, not only with our lips, but in our lives, by giving up ourselves to thy service, and by walking before thee in holiness and righteousness all our days; through Jesus Christ our Lord, to whom, with thee and the Holy Ghost, be all honor and glory, world without end. Amen.

The danger undoubtedly exists that a traditional form of words may be used lightly. People may recite the collect for the day with little or no thought of what they are saying. There is also the danger that the people may give little or no attention to what the minister is saying in free prayer. (What would be shown in a photograph taken of the congregation at the time of the pastoral prayer?) And there is the very real difficulty of following a prayer with which one is not familiar and at the same time directing the mind toward God. To give attention in two directions simultaneously, toward God and toward what is being said by the minister, is perhaps not impossible; but certainly it is not easy. More is demanded of those who are expected to use the pastoral prayer as a medium for their own approach to God than is required of those whose medium is a prayer they already know by heart.

Moreover, liturgical forms may serve to unite the people in a common act of worship. To this end hymns are deliberately used, especially in nonliturgical churches. And if hymns, why not prayers? The hymn:

> O God, our help in ages past,
> Our hope for years to come,

is no more appropriate or effective as a means of uniting a congregation than the collect:

Almighty God, unto whom all hearts are open, all desires known, and from whom no secrets are hid; cleanse the thoughts of our hearts by the inspiration of thy Holy Spirit, that we may perfectly love thee, and worthily magnify thy holy name; through Christ our Lord. Amen.

All this, however, does not necessarily mean that the nonliturgical church should abandon the practice of free prayer. The present demand in liturgical churches for Prayer Book revision may well give pause to anyone who wonders whether the day of the free prayer is past. Words and phrases become obsolete. Changes come over the face of the earth and the life of a people. New occasions arise, and new ideas, new concerns, new hopes. Unquestionably there is periodic need for Prayer Book revision. Yes, and there is the very real danger that such revision, even when imperatively called for, may be long delayed or resisted. The petition, "We humbly beseech thee, of thy great goodness, to restrain those immoderate rains, wherewith thou hast afflicted us," may seem out of place in a modern prayer book, but it is still to be found in *The Book of Common Prayer!* Free prayer is immediately adaptable to a given situation. And, what is more, it admits of an intimacy not otherwise attainable, so that it may serve to beget in a worshiping congregation a most blessed sense of the reality and presence of God.

Both formal prayer and free prayer have their dangers. The danger of formal prayer is that it may become a parrotlike recitation of words whose meaning and intention go unrecognized. The danger of free prayer is that it may be woefully inadequate. Hence the historical alternation between liturgical and nonliturgical worship. Let formal prayer become lifeless, and there is a Puritan Revolution. Let free prayer become slovenly and thoughtless, and there is a demand for the "enrichment of worship." But there is, I am convinced, need for both liturgic and nonliturgic prayer. I am prepared to endorse the statement:

Whatever its deficiencies, the Prayer Book is a repository of the best of the past. It represents not the passing mood of the moment, but the durable experience of the Church of the ages. . . . It releases the congregation from the affliction of individual idiosyncrasy. It affords prayers for all kinds of persons, and for all the manifold issues of life, because it has grown from the common experience of all. It is balanced, stable, conveying by its very form the changeless strength of God.[1]

I am also prepared to believe that in public worship there has been, is, and always will be a place for the pastoral prayer.

Evelyn Underhill, in discussing liturgical elements in worship, writes:

A certain restraint . . . is characteristic of all good liturgical action; for it exists to express the common worship of the family, not the fervour of the individual soul. Therefore the individual who prays from within the liturgy has to sacrifice something of his own will and feeling to the corporate movement; must submit to the ritual discipline, and lose his own prayer in that of the fellowship.[2]

This holds true of the pastoral prayer, whose true intention is to voice *the needs of the people*. The story is told of Father Taylor of the Sea-

[1] Edward Lambe Parsons and Bayard Hale Jones, *The American Prayer Book* (New York: Charles Scribner's Sons, 1937), pp. 9, 10.

[2] *Worship* (New York: Harper & Bros., 1937), p. 110.

15

men's Bethel in Boston that one night he came
to the mission and, having in mind a bereaved
family on whom he had just called, prayed:
"Lord, we are a poor widow with six children."
That was a real pastoral prayer. The minister in
public prayer is a priest presenting before God
the common need of forgiveness, of cleansing
and comfort, of guidance and help, of self-com-
mitment to the divine purpose, of faith and hope
and courage and strength.

Free prayer must not be free in the sense that
it is offered on the spur of the moment without
previous thought or with only such thought as
may be given to it after the service begins. Who
without previous preparation can present before
God the unspoken supplications of the people,
and this in words capable of directing attention
toward God? It is difficult enough to compose
between Sundays a prayer suitable for use in
public worship. It is very nearly impossible to
form such a prayer on the spur of the moment.
We have once or twice in a lifetime, perhaps,
heard a purely extemporary prayer that begot in
us a most wonderful sense of the reality and
presence of God. We would be well advised,
however, to assume that we, at least, are incapable
of so great an achievement and must make faithful preparation for the opportunity given us in
public prayer. On the opposite assumption there is
the very real danger that we may fail to minister
to our people at the level of their deepest need.

16

Public prayer no less than private should be addressed to God. This observation may seem superfluous, but apparently it is not. I have myself heard or read prayers whose object, it would seem, was to inform or exhort the congregation. One such prayer began with the statement: "Once again we are met in this hospitable room, folk of many families who through the week walk our several ways, but once a week gather here to unite our hearts and blend our voices in prayer and praise," and continued: "Some are here from force of habit; some, perchance, as a tiresome duty or act of condescension; others, it may be, drawn by some nameless need, seek here what they have been unable to find elsewhere; others are come because they love to be here, because to them there is no music so sweet as the songs of Zion, no hour of the week so satisfying as this, when they can have about them a company of Christian folk, can humbly and reverently bow before their Maker." As a lecture on the duty and privilege of church attendance, with slight digs at some among those present, this is pretty good. The only question is whether it is a prayer. And what of the minister who prayed: "Lead us to understand that we are all brothers. For are we not all brothers in the flesh? Are we not all born alike? Do we not all hunger alike and all suffer from the same ills of the flesh, and in the end all alike face death? And are we not all one in the divine spirit within

17

our flesh? Do we not all alike know the thrill of beauty, of goodness, of love, and the inspiration of religious uplift, whatsoever be the color of our skin, whatsoever be the land of our birth?" This brother was preaching, not praying; and that his eloquent argument helped anyone in the congregation to pray is surely open to doubt.

Even in public prayer there is no need to give information to God! In a pastoral prayer offered shortly before the outbreak of World War II, God was told: "The evils which have cursed us as a nation are being revealed in their true nature, and the implications of democracy, freedom, brotherhood, and justice as they exist in the divine mind are being burned into the consciousness of a growing number." This doubtless was news to God, though hardly in the sense of fresh and accurate information. It may, moreover, be doubted that God needs to be told: "Some of us are disappointed. Our fondest desires have failed of realization and our brightest hopes have vanished like a mirage in the desert. Instead of triumphantly marching along the sunpath of glorious achievement, our lot has been to tread the trivial round of common care." We may well suppose that there is not much about us that is quite unknown to God.

The pastoral prayer need not be long. It need not be as long as a sermon or even a sermonette. If it is more than three hundred words, it is probably too long, unless it consists of a number of collects separated from one another by a congregational or choral amen. A long, rambling prayer ceases after a while to be common prayer and becomes only a monologue in which the pastor himself, as he rambles on, may be more concerned with sentence structure than with anything else. The sustained attention necessary for real prayer is not easy to accomplish even in the privacy of one's own room, much less in a situation where, as in the case of the pastoral prayer, the mind of the worshiper must move simultaneously in two directions—toward God and toward what is being said by the minister. To offer a free prayer of many more than three hundred words is almost certainly to ask too much of the congregation. Even a three-hundred-word prayer is longer than the longest prayer in *The Book of Common Prayer* outside of the Order for the Administration of Holy Communion; and in the case of the Prayer Book the worshiper has the advantage of prior acquaintance with what is being said.

The choice of words in public prayer is a matter of the greatest importance. Those words are suitable, and those alone, which serve to lift mind and heart toward God. Unsuitable are words such as "ideology," phrases such as "the lure of short cuts," clichés such as "freedom's altar." This is the language of the classroom or the soapbox, not the language of prayer. In general, Anglo-Saxon words are to be preferred to Greek or Latin derivatives. Words like "bread," "work," "world," "light," "truth" may more certainly be depended upon to lift mind and heart to God than words like "sustenance," "employment," "universe," "illumination," "veracity," which have far less power to reach the depths of the soul. Technical words not "understanded of the people" have, of course, no place in prayer. And I for one should question the propriety of phrases such as "labor movement," "production for use," "co-operative commonwealth," which have different meanings for different men, and are less likely to bring the soul to repentance and self-dedication than to produce feelings of irritation or self-satisfaction, depending upon the social status of the congregation. Most unsuitable are forms of expression that call attention to the minister and provoke wonder at his eloquence or (as some may view it) his exhibitionism. If the minister in prayer alludes to "the wave-tossed surface of our wind-driven life," or to "the last loving haven from the loneliness of life," or to "a morning glorious, alight with the brightness of resurrection and the promise of a day of opportunity," then he may be sure that the people are thinking about *him*, though not entirely sure what they are thinking. Here the problem is not only intellectual but moral and spiritual as well. Basically it is the problem of self-forgetting.

Adjectives in prayer should be most sparingly used. The temptation to use them may be great;

they afford the opportunity of eloquence or what passes for eloquence among the undiscerning. But they are mischievous if they are many, as indeed they are in sermons. They slow down a prayer whose true mission is to lead the people to the throne of grace. Worse still, they get in the way of the people's approach to God, attracting attention to themselves, like persons flashily dressed. Consider, for example, the prayer: "Grant that we may meet the *haunting* need of these *terrible* days of judgment with such *compelling* courage and *matchless* loyalties as shall make thy people invincible against all the barriers of darkness, evil, and inertia." (Italics mine.) And note in comparison the prayer:

O God, who rulest the world from end to end and from everlasting to everlasting; speak to our hearts when courage fails, and men faint from fear, and the love of many grows cold, and there is distress of the nations on earth. Keep us resolute and steadfast in the things that cannot be shaken, abounding in hope and knowing that our labor is not vain in thee. Restore our faith in the omnipotence of good; renew the love which never fails; and make us to lift up our eyes and behold, beyond the things which are seen and temporal, the things which are unseen and eternal. Amen.

These two prayers have the same objective; but the first is derailed by obstructing adjectives, whereas the second, with strong nouns and verbs,

21

carries the soul to the eternal source of courage and strength. It is worthy of note that the prayers of the ages contain but few adjectives—the greatest of all, only one.

The native language of prayer is the language of poetry. Only the language of poetry can adequately convey the reality of eternal God: "Lord, thou hast been our dwelling place in all generations." Or the reality of human creatureship: "Know ye that the Lord he is God: it is he that hath made us, and not we ourselves; we are his people, and the sheep of his pasture." Or the soul's need and plea for forgiveness: "Create in me a clean heart, O God; and renew a right spirit within me." Or the confidence of the trusting soul: "Yea, though I walk through the valley of the shadow of death, I will fear no evil; for thou art with me." Or the soul's invincible surmise: "And he shall wipe away every tear from their eyes; and death shall be no more; neither shall there be mourning, nor crying, nor pain, any more: the former things are passed away."

Not all God's preachers are poets. And what is one to do if one is not? Being myself a preacher who is not a poet or a poet's son, I have found it necessary and most helpful to steep my mind in the Psalms, in Isaiah, and in *The Book of Common Prayer*. This practice I recommend to anyone whose mental processes are similarly prosaic. It is not, of course, a substitute for the

22

divine gift of poetry; but it may serve to induce
the mood and to some extent even the manner of
poetry, so that the prayer thus resulting will have
some correspondence with what is true and good
in the public worship of God.

Occasionally the pastoral prayer may well take
the literary structure of the collect. This prayer
form is not easy to master.

It is coming to be realized that a Collect, presenting
a single profound and universal petition within its
brief compass, is as exacting an art-form as a sonnet.
It is free poetry, where thoughts, instead of words,
rhyme in definite strophe-patterns.[3]

But the art of making collects is worth cultivat-
ing, for the collect at its best has the virtue of
unity, of conciseness, of enduring grace and
strength. A collect may consist of a single sentence. It must not express more than one main
desire or thought. (A prayer containing several
different and unrelated petitions is not a collect.)
Often, but not always, a collect has five parts:
the address to God; a relative clause setting forth
the divine attribute in virtue of which the prayer
is offered; the petition or thanksgiving; a final
clause indicating the purpose or end for which
the divine action is sought; and a formal con-
clusion. For example, a familiar collect for guidance has the structure:

[3] Parsons and Jones, *op. cit.*, p. 144.

Invocation:	O God,
Relative clause:	by whom the meek are guided in judgment, and light riseth up in darkness for the godly;
Petition:	grant us, in all our doubts and uncertainties, the grace to ask what thou wouldest have us to do;
Purpose:	that the spirit of wisdom may save us from all false choices, and that in thy light we may see light, and in thy straight path may not stumble;
Ending:	through Jesus Christ our Lord. Amen.

A somewhat different pattern appears in the collect:

Grant, we beseech thee, merciful Lord, to thy faithful people pardon and peace, that we may be cleansed from all our sins, and serve thee with a quiet mind; through Jesus Christ our Lord. Amen.

And still another in the collect:

Almighty God, we beseech thee with thy gracious favor to behold our universities, colleges, and schools, that knowledge may be increased among us, and all good learning flourish and abound. Bless all who teach and all who learn, and grant that in humility of heart they may ever look unto thee, who art the fountain of all wisdom; through Jesus Christ our Lord. Amen.

The collect ordinarily is a short prayer—too short to serve as a "pastoral" prayer. But the pastoral prayer may well begin with a petition or thanksgiving cast in the collect mold, and may also close with a collect.

Occasionally, too, the pastoral prayer may follow the pattern of a litany. The litany form was used in Christian worship at a very early date, as far back, probably, as the first part of the fourth century. It seems that the pastoral prayer in those days was frequently interrupted by fervent ejaculations from the congregation, and that the litany was devised to bring some semblance of order to the service.[4] Here, in any case, is a prayer form of extraordinary promise. Its possibilities may be seen in the modern prayer "Thanksgiving and Litany for the Missionary Work of the Church," which says in part:

Thanks be to thee, most glorious God, Father, Son, and Holy Spirit, for the revelation of thyself in this our world, and for thy commission to thy Church to proclaim the gospel of Christ to every creature.

Thanks be to thee, O God.

For the early disciples who were sent forth by Christ to proclaim the coming of the kingdom,

We praise thee, O God.

For the apostles of the nations, who in obedience to his word carried the gospel through the world,

We praise thee, O God.

[4] *Ibid.*, pp. 125 ff.

25

For those missionaries, known and unknown, who first brought the gospel to these shores,

We praise thee, O God.

For all the faithful, who, in ages of darkness, kept their lamps burning and watched for the coming of the Lord,

We praise thee, O God.

For all who at any time have recalled the Church to her great task of evangelizing the world,

We praise thee, O God.

For those who have gone to the ends of the world with the joyful news, and have sought out the dark places of the earth to bring light to them that dwell in the shadow of death,

We praise thee, O God.

For thy missionary servants who have joined the noble army of martyrs, and for all converts to the faith who have sealed their testimony with their blood,

We praise thee, O God.

For the innumerable company who now praise thy name out of every kindred and nation and tongue,

We praise thee, O God. Alleluia. Amen.

We acknowledge, O Lord, that we have proved unworthy of thy mercies, and confess how little we have done to hand on, in freedom and fullness, the faith which was brought to us through many perils and purchased with such pain. And the Church's long neglect of this, her bounden duty,

O Lord, forgive.

26

Our unchristian example at home revealed to the world in our racial prejudices, our narrow nationalism, our wars, and our slums,

O Lord, forgive.

We do beseech thee to hear us, O Lord, that thou wouldst stir up the hearts of thy faithful people to greater obedience, and unite thy Church to face the world's great need, and that thou wouldst send forth laborers into thy harvest,

Hear us, we beseech thee.

The pastoral prayer may take the litany form, for it is surely defensible that the minister should offer *both* the petition or thanksgiving *and* the appropriate response. Thus in the litany given above the minister might proceed as follows: "For the early disciples who were sent forth by Christ to proclaim the coming of the kingdom; for the apostles of the nations, who in obedience to his word carried the gospel through the world; for the missionaries, known and unknown, who first brought the gospel to these shores, we praise thee, O God. For all the faithful, who, in ages of darkness, kept their lamps burning and watched for the coming of the Lord, . . . we praise and bless thy holy name."

It would be easy for the minister in the non-liturgical church simply to "lift" collects or litanies from a prayer book. But this would be a surrender to laziness and a deplorable repudiation of a great tradition. The church needs, in addition to the "prayers of the ages," prayers immediately relevant to the contemporary situation and voiced in the living language of the day. The minister in the nonliturgical church may well feel called of God to pay the price, intellectual and spiritual, of effective pastoral prayer.

I

General Prayers

Eternal God, who hast been our dwelling place in all generations; we rejoice that neither life nor death is able to separate us from thee.

When we are tempted, thou art at hand to warn us and to provide a way of escape.

When we sin, thy presence is not withdrawn but thy Holy Spirit works without ceasing to bring us to repentance and to cleanse us from all unrighteousness.

When we suffer the loss of earthly possessions or are any way distressed, thou art our comfort and our unfailing stay.

When the world about us is full of darkness and tumult, it is in thy light that we see light and by thy strength that we are upheld all the day long.

When we go forth to battle against the forces of evil, thou art the faith that arms us and the grace that sees us through.

When we are separated from those we love, thy presence unites us with them in bonds which no distance can sever and which death itself cannot break.

When we are shut in by old age or illness, thy angels come and minister unto us.

When we are left alone, yet are we not alone, for thou, O Father, art with us; and when our work on earth is done, thou art our hope and our resurrection.

O God, our help in ages past and our eternal home, into thy hands we commend our spirits; through Jesus Christ our Lord. AMEN.

O THOU whose mercy is over all, we beseech thee for our brethren in every place, and most especially for those who are in any way distressed.

Visit the sick with thy comfort and healing power. Come to the bereaved with thy peace, and increase in them the faith that love is stronger than death. Hasten with thy protection to those who are sorely tempted; make them strong to resist and conquer. Draw near to all who are lonely, all who are anxious, all who are cast down and discouraged, and to those who suffer in the suffering of those they

Your Help Please!

Did this book meet your expectations? If so, why?
If not, please criticize.

A BOOK OF PASTORAL PRAYERS

Please tell us what advertisement, review, or display in-fluenced you to buy this book and from what source you bought it.

NAME————————————————————————————————
Your address is unnecessary; buy from your own book-seller!

WE PAY POSTAGE. SIMPLY FILL OUT AND MAIL WITHOUT STAMP.

ABINGDON-COKESBURY PRESS   *150 Fifth Ave.*
New York 11, N. Y.

love, that they may be strengthened with all power for all endurance and patience.

Look in thy might upon those who have no helper. Defend the poor, and save the children of the needy. Make haste for the relief of those who know the pains of hunger and those who have nowhere to lay their head. Bring near the deliverance of those who are persecuted and those who are discriminated against, exploited, and oppressed. Show thy compassion to every victim of injustice, and to those who inflict loss and pain upon others show the demands of thy righteousness and the inexorable working of thy holy laws.

Reveal unto us, we beseech thee, those things in ourselves which are adding to the sum of human misery. Help us to repent of these our sins, and give us grace to consecrate ourselves to thy service, that we may be used of thee to help one another and to set forward thy blessed kingdom; through Jesus Christ our Lord. AMEN.

ETERNAL GOD, who hast been our dwelling in all generations; our fathers cried unto thee, and thou didst hear them and deliver them from all their fears. They looked unto thee, trusting in thy mercy, and thy Spirit upheld them all their days. Give us to know that, as thou wast with those who came before us, so art thou also with us to save and guide and bless. Uphold us in the hour of temptation; keep our feet from falling, and guide them into the way of thy peace. Strengthen us to bear loss or pain or grievous disappointment; support and enable us by the might of thy Spirit, that we may not fail nor be afraid. Deliver us from envy, hate, and selfishness; give us grace to act as becometh thy children, helping one another and forbearing one another in love. Make us servants of thy compassion, to raise the fallen, to relieve the distressed, to promote peace and good will among men; till at length by thy great mercy we enter the company of thy prophets and saints who dwell with thee evermore; through Jesus Christ our Lord. AMEN.

O GOD, most merciful and gracious, by the might of thy Spirit lift us to thy presence, that we may receive mercy and find grace to help us in time of need.

Thou knowest the sins which we have all committed against thee. Have mercy upon us, O thou who art kind toward the unthankful and evil. Turn us to thee in hearty repentance, that thou mayest forgive us our sins and cleanse us from all unrighteousness.

Thou knowest the fears and anxieties that oppress us. Teach us to put our trust in thee and not be afraid. When our way is hard, give us to know that thou art with us, and that with thee is help adequate to our need. When the spirit is willing but the flesh is weak, bestow upon us thy special grace, that we may not falter in our trust but continue steadfast to the end. When we are fearful for those we love, grant that we may commit them to thine unfailing love and care, asking that thou wilt work in both them and us thy perfect will.

O thou sole source of life and hope, draw us unto thyself more and more, that we may not lose heart nor wander from thy ways, but may in thee find healing for our hurt, strength for our pilgrimage, and that peace within which thou alone canst give; through Jesus Christ our Lord. Amen.

O GOD, whose mercies cannot be numbered; we raise to thee our grateful praise.

For the glory of sunrise and sunset, for shelter and raiment and daily bread, for work that wins livelihood and the sense of belonging, for the blessings of family life and for good neighbors and friends, we give thee thanks.

For joys that hearten and refresh us, for afflictions that bring new insights and readier understanding and compassion, for the trials whereby we are tested and for the power to triumph over disaster, we give thee thanks.

Above all, we thank thee for thyself, O thou whose faithfulness is unto all generations. For the love wherewith thou lovest us, despite our neglect, ingratitude, and sin, and for thy guiding hand upon us and thy watchful care over us throughout the whole course of our life, we praise and bless thy glorious name.

O Father of mercies and God of all comfort, grant us thy grace, that we who have received mercy may also show mercy and, in gratitude to thee, do all we can for one another; through Jesus Christ our Lord. AMEN.

O GOD OF GRACE, who hast called us to thine eternal glory in Christ our Lord; we praise and bless thy glorious name.

To see thee is to find meaning in life.

To obtain thy forgiveness is healing and peace.

To be thy servant is perfect freedom.

To meditate upon thy purpose and power is enduring hope.

To love and trust thee is to face life and death unafraid.

O heavenly Father, whom to know is life eternal; in thy great mercy open our eyes to thy glory and incline our hearts to do thy will; through Jesus Christ our Lord. AMEN.

O GOD, who hast taught us that in quietness and in confidence shall be our strength; make us to know that thou art with us, and that with thee is help adequate to our need.

We come to thee with our sins, asking thy forgiveness.

We come with our anxieties, needing courage and confidence such as are born of trust in thee.

35

We come with our manifold problems, knowing that wisdom dwells in thee, and that only in thy light shall we see light.

We come with our griefs, in the assurance that thou art able to revive the fainting soul and to comfort those who are crushed.

O thou who knowest us altogether and art acquainted with all our ways, show to us thy mercy and the wonders of thy grace. Grant us peace within our hearts. Grant us light upon our way. Grant us strength sufficient for the work we have to do and the burdens we have to bear. Enable us to fight the good fight, to endure to the end, and to obtain the victory; through Jesus Christ our Lord. AMEN.

O GOD, from whom every family in heaven and on earth is named; visit, we beseech thee, the homes of thy people, and let thy presence establish them in peace.

Be with those who are joined together in holy wedlock. Let thy Spirit deliver them from all evil, and make them strong to endure the trials and tensions of this earthly life. Fill them with the love that never fails; and unite them ever more closely to thee and to one another in the bonds of faith, loyalty, and devotion.

Be with all fathers and mothers. Endue them with patience and understanding; give to them strength sufficient for the day; and so assist them by thy counsel that they may bring up their whole family in thy faith and peace.

Bless, we beseech thee, the children given into our keeping. Be thou their guide and stay. Open their eyes to the way of life, and incline their hearts to do thy will; that they may be saved from all false views and choices; and that, committing themselves to thee, they may bring to completion their gifts and powers and find in thy service great reward. All which we ask in the name of thy Son, Jesus Christ our Lord. AMEN.

O GOD, who hast taught us by thy blessed Son that we ought always to pray and not lose heart; we look to thee for the help which thou alone canst give.

We who are weary and heavy-laden would find rest in thee.

We who have sinned would obtain thy forgiveness, thy healing, and thy peace.

We who are confused and sorely tempted would be led of thy wisdom and upheld in thy strength.

We who are anxious for the morrow would know that neither things present nor things to come shall be able to separate us from thee, whose grace is sufficient for us.

We who dwell in a world of insecurity would have within a sense of security which the world cannot give nor take away.

We who know the anguish of bereavement would know also the hope of joyous reunion in a world where death shall be no more.

Give us grace to put our whole trust in thee. Enable us to go forth each day in the confidence that thou art with us amid the storms and troubles of life, and that with thee is forgiveness for sin, help for pain, strength for the day, and peace at the last; through Jesus Christ our Lord. AMEN.

ETERNAL GOD, our heavenly Father, who art the source of our life and the end of our pilgrimage; we praise and bless thee for thy presence with us all our days. Thou dost satisfy us in the morning with thy lovingkindness; thou dost uphold us at noonday in the strength of thy Spirit; and when the evening comes, thou art our hope and our rest.

Make us to remember thy goodness toward us in past years, the lovingkindness and tender mercies bestowed upon us from the days of our youth, that we may not be anxious and fearful but may be upheld, now and always, by sure trust in thee. Let the knowledge of thy presence support us, in health and in sickness, in joy and in sorrow, in hope fulfilled and in hope denied, in the midst of life and in the hour of death.

Put far from us, we beseech thee, all things whatsoever that hide from us thy blessed face and leave us unaware of thy presence; and in thy great mercy receive us into thy service. Purify our motives; deepen our understanding; quicken our hearts; and give to us such strength of mind and body as may enable us for the work to which thou dost call us; that we may have a part in thy great redemption and enter at the last into thy peace; through Jesus Christ our Lord. AMEN.

O THOU who art the source of all light and hope, make us to know our constant need of thee.

Without thee we run into folly and bring disaster upon ourselves and our children.

Without thee we have no defense before the assault of temptation, or against the storms and troubles of life.

Without thee we are left at the last with none to uphold us before the awful mystery of life and death.

Fill us, O Lord, with unending desire for thee, that thou mayest make thyself known to us and bestow upon us the manifold blessings of thy grace; through Jesus Christ our Lord. AMEN.

ETERNAL FATHER, who art in every place to save and bless; we beseech thee for our brethren in all parts of the world. Show thy mercy upon all who cry to thee for succor. Look in thy compassion upon all who have sinned and are receiving the due reward of their deeds; give them to know that thou art good and ready to forgive and plenteous in mercy unto them that call upon thee. Draw near to all who are in sickness, trouble, or sorrow; that they may be upheld and comforted; and that, trusting in thee, they may have hope both for this life and for the life to come. Have in thy special care the hungry, the homeless, all who are persecuted or oppressed, all who are wrongfully accused and condemned, and all little children who are victims of man's greed and violence; receive them into thy protection, we beseech thee, and come mightily to their aid.

We confess with shame our own part in the world's undoing. We have cherished the ambitions of pride and greed. We have put self-interest before all other considerations. We have kept silence in the presence of wrong and injustice, indifferent to the fate of others or afraid for our own security. Oh forgive us, we pray thee, the harm we have done; and in thy great mercy bring us into allegiance to thy purpose of good for mankind. All which we ask through Jesus Christ our Lord, to whom be glory for ever and ever. AMEN.

ETERNAL FATHER, who hast made us for thyself, so that our heart knows no rest till it rests in thee; we thy needy children plead for the help which thou alone canst give.

Be thou our fortress in the hour of temptation, an house of defense to save us.

Be thou our light when the day is dark and we know not which way to turn.

Be thou our strength when the flesh is weak and the spirit sore troubled and depressed.

Be thou our courage in the hour of danger and in the day of adversity.

Be thou our assurance when those we love are taken from our sight and thou alone canst uphold and comfort us.

Be thou our hope when our own hopes fail and but for thee we should give way to despair.

Be thou at all times our help and our salvation, until at length by thy great mercy we win the victory over sin and death, and come to everlasting life; through Jesus Christ our Lord. AMEN.

O ETERNAL GOD, thou sole refuge of the children of men, suffer us not to fall away from thee. Apart from thee we know no rest but are anxious and fearful. Unmindful of thee we run into folly and bring disaster upon ourselves and our children. Oh make haste, we beseech thee, to save us. In thy mercy deliver us from false ideas and ambitions, from purposes and policies that are contrary to thy peace, and from foolish trust in our own powers. Turn us to thee in hearty repentance and true humility, that thou mayest forgive all our iniquities, and heal all our diseases, and redeem our life from destruction; through Jesus Christ our Lord. AMEN.

ETERNAL GOD, the unfailing source of light and mercy, we praise and bless thee for thy great power and goodness.

In time of trouble thou art our refuge and strength.

In our day of trial thou art our deliverance from temptation and from despair.

When we walk in darkness and have no light upon the questions that torment us, still may we rest our minds on thee, knowing that thou hast the answer to all our problems.

In our day of sorrow when we walk alone thou art our companion, our comfort, and our hope.

Teach us to love thee with all our heart and mind and strength, and to love our friends in thee and our enemies for thy sake. Give to us such a measure of thy Spirit that we may be used of thee to restore the penitent, to comfort the sorrowing, to relieve the suffering, and to bring faith and hope to many; through Jesus Christ our Lord. AMEN.

O LORD, heavenly Father, almighty and ever-lasting God, we heartily rejoice in thee.

We rejoice that thou art God, and that thy years shall have no end.

We rejoice that thou sharest the life of thy human children, bearing with them the burden of their frailty, their sinful wanderings and sorrows, and the suffering without which they cannot be made perfect.

We rejoice that thy righteousness will not let us sin with impunity, and that thine is the power to forgive all our iniquities and to heal all our diseases.

We rejoice that thou dost never take thy Holy Spirit from us but dost follow us with thy mercy and saving help throughout the whole course of our life.

We rejoice that the issues of life and death

belong to thee, and that in everything thou dost work with those who love thee to bring about what is good.

We rejoice in the work that is ours to do, in which we have the opportunity of a part in thy glorious work of creation and redemption.

O thou with whom is fullness of joy, deliver us, we beseech thee, from faithless fear and anxiety. Send us forth each day in the confidence that thou art with us; and teach us to trust thee always, that thy peace, which passes all understanding, may guard our hearts and our thoughts and bring us to everlasting life; through Jesus Christ our Lord. AMEN.

O GOD most merciful and gracious, we turn to thee for the help which thou alone canst give.

Thou who takest away the sins of the world, by the might of thy Spirit lift us, we pray thee, to thy presence, that in nearness to thee we may obtain deliverance from thoughts that weaken and defile, from evil desires and imaginations, from selfishness, meanness, and pettiness, and from all unfaithfulness and cowardice.

Thou who makest light to shine out of darkness, lighten our path and shine in our hearts; that we may see the way we should go; and that, being saved from false ambitions and choices, we may walk in thy light and fulfill thy good purpose for us.

Thou who art able to do exceeding abundantly above all that we ask or think, put away from us worry and every anxious fear. Send us forth each day in the confidence that thou art with us, and that thy grace, if we trust thee, will see us through.

Draw near to all who are sorely tempted, all who are anxious and fearful, all who are confused and troubled, all who are hard bestead; that, knowing that thou art with them, they may fear no evil; and that, by thy blessing upon them, they may come off more than conqueror; through Jesus Christ our Lord. AMEN.

O GOD, our help in ages past, our hope for years to come, we raise to thee our grateful praise. With thee is deliverance from sin and despair, and unfailing help in trouble. Thou hast the answer to all our problems, and in thy will is our peace.

We come before thee as sinful men in need of thy forgiveness. Have mercy upon us, O thou whose mercy endureth forever. Blot out our transgressions, and cleanse us from our sins. By the might of thy Spirit renew and strengthen us, and enable us for the work we have to do.

We would unburden our hearts before thee, voicing our griefs, our disappointments, our secret fears, and the longings that save to thee we dare not name. O thou who knowest us altogether and art acquainted with all our ways, in thy great compassion grant unto us such comfort and encouragement as thou seest we are in need of.

We look to thee for guidance amid the perplexities and perils of our time. O thou in whom wisdom dwelleth, give us grace to listen to what thou hast to say, that we may not be blinded by fear or by self-interest, but in thy light may see the way we should go and what we must do to be saved; through Jesus Christ our Lord. AMEN.

O GOD OF GRACE, who art ever with us and never more regardful of us than when in our anxiety or pain we question thy providence; we raise to thee our grateful praise.

Make us to recognize our dependence upon thee, our constant need of thy forgiveness, thy guidance, and thy saving help. And we beseech thee, make us aware of thy presence; give us to know that thou art with us, and that with thee we are able for anything.

We do not ask for immunity from all loss and pain, knowing that suffering may teach us much, and that we are called to serve thy purpose of good regardless of cost to ourselves. But give us wisdom and courage sufficient for the day, and such measure of mental and bodily strength as may enable us for the work we have to do; and we beseech thee, increase our faith, that we may abound in thy service and know that our labor in thee is not in vain.

Let thy Spirit mightily work throughout all the world; that men and women everywhere may turn to thee for forgiveness, guidance, and help; and that so thy healing may spring forth speedily and thy kingdom be set forward; through Jesus Christ our Lord. AMEN.

O THOU who dwellest in the high and holy place and with him also that is of a contrite and humble spirit, we praise and bless thee for thy presence with us all our days.

When we are tempted, thou dost seek to restrain and deliver us.

When we do what is wrong and get into trouble, thou dost call us to repentance and give us the opportunity of a new start in life.

In time of trouble, when we know not where to turn, thou dost come to us with thy comfort and thy saving help.

When we pray, it is thou who dost prompt us, seeking to bring us into fellowship with thyself, that, staying our minds on thee, we may see the way we should go and obtain courage and strength for our pilgrimage.

Grant us now, we beseech thee, the healing of thy forgiveness, the unfailing light of thy counsel, the upholding assurance of thy presence. And when thou hast renewed our strength, send us forth as thy servants to do what we can for others and to improve the conditions of the world; through Jesus Christ our Lord. AMEN.

II

Prayers for Certain Days in the Christian Year

First Sunday in Advent

O MERCIFUL GOD, who didst come in Jesus Christ with saving power to a world that walked in darkness and in the shadow of death; we praise and bless thee for all those thy servants who helped prepare the way for his appearing, and for those who received him and gave to him the homage of their hearts and lives. For prophets who in the face of tyranny declared thy truth and thy righteousness, for psalmists who in days of gloom still believed in thy great goodness and sang praises unto thy name, and for innumerable simple folk who waited in patience and unfailing hope for the manifestation of thy glory, we raise to thee our grateful praise. Grant, we beseech thee, that we in this time may show forth thy salvation. Help us to put away all untruthfulness and all selfishness and greed, all malice and prejudice and cowardice. Let thy Holy Spirit cleanse us from all our sins, and teach us to love one another even as thou dost love us, that we may make manifest in our lives what thou canst do for thy faithful people; through Jesus Christ our Lord. AMEN.

Second Sunday in Advent

ETERNAL FATHER, whose coming in Jesus Christ for our salvation was promised beforehand through inspired prophets; we praise and bless thee for the gracious words which thou hast spoken through those thy servants who apprehended thy truth and thy righteousness, and set forth thy glory in unfading scriptures for our guidance and comfort. Forgive us, we beseech thee, if we have neglected thy revelation and wandered into folly. Turn us again to thy holy Word; that we may have a lamp for our feet, a light on our path; and that, by remaining steadfast and drawing encouragement from the Scriptures, we may cherish hope both for this life and for the life to come; through Jesus Christ our Lord. AMEN.

Third Sunday in Advent

O GOD, who through faithful men didst prepare the way for thy coming in Jesus Christ

to save us from our sins and bring us to everlasting life; grant that we also, in this time, may
prepare thy way before thee, that thy kingdom
may come with power and in great glory. Suffer
us not to be discouraged by the present conditions of the world, or by the afflictions and disappointments of life. And forbid that we should
grow weary in well-doing. Make us to know
that thy purpose of good is beyond defeat, and
grant to us such a measure of thy patience that
we may persevere in thy service and, by thy
great love, bring healing and hope to others;
through Jesus Christ our Lord. AMEN.

Fourth Sunday in Advent

O ETERNAL GOD, the creator and preserver of
all mankind, who carest for thy human
children of every race and nation; make haste,
we beseech thee, to help us, for our transgressions have overtaken us; we are compassed about
with many and great evils, till we know not
where to turn. Look upon us in thy compassion,
and come speedily to our aid. Bring us to repentance for the sins which we have all committed
against thee, that thou mayest forgive us our
sins, and form a right spirit within us, and guide

our feet into the way of peace. Put to shame those who would make darkness to be light and light to be darkness. Confound those in whom lust for wealth or power is threatening the world with new disasters. Open the eyes of those who are blinded by ignorance, fear, or prejudice. In thy great mercy bring good tidings to the poor, heal the brokenhearted, set at liberty the oppressed, and fill with rejoicing all workers of good. Let the whole earth be filled with thy praise, O Lord, heavenly Father, almighty and everlasting God; and unto thee be glory and majesty, dominion and power, both now and forever. AMEN.

Christmas Day

O GOD OUR FATHER, who at this time didst give thy blessed Son that we, through him, should not perish but have eternal life; we raise to thee our grateful praise. For the light of thy truth and the knowledge of thy glory, for the faith and love and hope whereby a multitude out of every race and nation have been renewed and blessed, and for the joy and gladness with which thy wondrous gift has filled our hearts, we give thee humble thanks.

Grant, we beseech thee, that we at this holy time may be cleansed from all our sins. Put far from us every evil desire, every selfish ambition, and all hate, uncharitableness, and bitterness. Form in us more and more the likeness of Christ, that we may enter into thy peace and be used of thee to establish peace in all the earth. Look in thy compassion upon those who are now in sorrow and affliction. Make them to know that thou art with them, and that with thee there is comfort and hope. And we beseech thee, grant unto all men at this Christmas time the manifold blessings of thy grace; through Jesus Christ our Lord. AMEN.

O GOD OF GRACE, who didst give Jesus Christ to be our Saviour; we beseech thee to overcome our darkness with his light, our fears with his faith, our selfishness with his love, our indolence and cowardice with his steadfast devotion, that we may live ever as in thy presence, and perform faithfully our appointed tasks, and finally come to everlasting life; through the same Jesus Christ our Lord. AMEN.

Sunday After Christmas

O GOD, who hast given us grace at this time to celebrate the birth of thy beloved Son Jesus; we praise and bless thee for the faith and hope that he has brought unto us and for the many blessings of these holy days. For reunited families, for the love and devotion of kindred and friends, for the light and laughter, the beauty, joy, good will, and peace that at Christmas time prevail, we raise to thee our grateful praise. O thou who didst draw near in Jesus Christ to make thyself known to us and to work for our good, suffer us not to doubt thee in the coming days. Forbid that we should give way to worry and faithless fears. Help us to put our whole trust in thee, not questioning thy providence even in the darkest hour, but resting in the assurance that thou art with us and art able to do exceeding abundantly above all that we ask or think. And we beseech thee, give us grace each day to ask what thou wouldst have us to do; that in thy light we may see light and follow the way we should go; and that, fulfilling thy good purpose for us, we may comfort others with the comfort wherewith we ourselves have been comforted of thee, and have a part in thy great redemption; through Jesus Christ our Lord. Amen.

New Year's Eve

O GOD, before whose face the seasons change and the years pass; we beseech thee at this time to hear our prayer and let our cry come unto thee. We are weak and mortal men set amid the conditions of a passing world. Our days are as grass which in the morning flourishes and by evening fades and withers. O thou whose years shall have no end, our hope is in thee. Thou art the source of our life and the end of our pilgrimage. Thou art our refuge and strength, a very present help in trouble. In the world we have tribulation, but with thee there is rest and joy and peace. Continue thou thy mercy toward us, we humbly beseech thee. Forgive us the sins which we have committed in the past, and in thy perfect wisdom and love go with us into the days that are ahead. In the hour of temptation keep our feet from falling and guide them into the way of thy peace. In the day of testing uphold and direct us, that we may not fail nor be afraid. By the might of thy Spirit bring us into thy kingdom more and more; and grant that, working together with thee for the fulfillment of thy purpose of good, we may in thee abide, now in this time of our mortal life and in thy eternal kingdom for ever and ever; through Jesus Christ our Lord, in whose name we ascribe unto thee all honor and praise, world without end. AMEN.

The Epiphany, or the Manifestation of Christ to the Gentiles

O GOD, by whose light men from the east were led into the knowledge of thy blessed Son; send out thy light and thy truth into the east and the west, and into the north and the south; that all men everywhere may behold thy glory in the face of Jesus Christ; and that so thy kingdom may be set forward among the nations and thy peace be established in all the earth; through the same Jesus Christ our Lord. AMEN.

Ash Wednesday

O MERCIFUL GOD, who hast promised forgiveness to all those who confess and forsake their sins; make us to be heartily sorry for our misdoings, that thou mayest forgive all our iniquities, and heal all our diseases, and redeem our life from destruction. Put far from us the self-righteousness which has blinded our eyes, so that we do not see ourselves as sinful men in need of thy mercy. Take away the foolish pride and self-concern which make us to hurt one another and to add to the fear and confusion of the world. Mercifully deliver us from inordinate love of self and from every false ambition, and grant us the constant aid of thy Holy Spirit, that we may follow daily the path of righteousness and enter at the last into thy peace; through Jesus Christ our Lord. AMEN.

First Sunday in Lent

O GOD, whose blessed Son did fast forty days and forty nights in preparation for his holy mission; beget in us, we beseech thee, the same desire which was in him to learn and do thy will. Forbid that through indulgence of the flesh we should dim our vision of thee and render ourselves unfit for thy service. Give us grace to master our bodies and bring them into subjection to thy good purpose for us. Teach us by prayer and fasting to win self-control, that we may commit ourselves wholly to thee and enter more and more into thy blessed kingdom; through him who for our sake consecrated himself, Jesus Christ our Lord. AMEN.

Second Sunday in Lent

O GOD, whose beloved Son had compassion on the sick and healed their diseases; grant that his spirit may live and grow in us. Kindle within us a holy wrath toward social conditions that make life hard and barren for many, and injure them in both body and soul. Give us the will and power to abolish poverty, ignorance, and injustice, and to assure to all the people the opportunity of a life of health and joy. Lead us to new knowledge of the cause and cure of disease, and constrain us to make help for pain available to every son of man.

Bless all those thy servants who are engaged in the ministry of healing. Help them to walk worthily of the calling wherewith they were called. Give to them the spirit of wisdom and understanding; and let the children of men, even the least, be as precious in their sight as in thine. And above all that man can do for man, do thou, O heavenly Father, make manifest thy saving power; through Jesus Christ our Lord. AMEN.

Third Sunday in Lent

ETERNAL GOD, who in Jesus Christ didst speak words of truth for our guidance; let thy Holy Spirit bring to our remembrance the things he said: that we are to be pure in heart, abjuring lust and pride and insincerity; that we are to seek first thy kingdom and thy righteousness, trusting in thy wisdom and power; that we are to desire not to be ministered unto but to minister, following the way of thy greatness; that we are to love not only our friends but our enemies also, seeking good for all men, even as thou, O Father, makest thy sun to rise on the evil and the good, and sendest rain on the just and the unjust. Bring to our remembrance these and all other words that he spoke for our good, and give us grace to do them, that we may set forward thy blessed kingdom, and finally enter into thy peace; through the same Jesus Christ our Lord. AMEN.

Fourth Sunday in Lent

O GOD, whose blessed Son steadfastly set his face to go to the city where he was to suffer and die; let there be in us this same devotion which was in him. Forgive us, we beseech thee, our many evasions of duty. We have held back from fear of men. We have ranked security and comfort higher than justice and truth, and our hearts condemn us. But thou, O Lord, who art greater than our hearts, have mercy upon us. Purge us from the fear that is born of self-concern. Beget in us the fear that we may be found wanting in loyalty to thee and thy purpose of good for mankind. Fill us with the compassion of him who for our sake endured the cross; that we may be delivered from selfishness and cowardice; and that, dedicating our lives to thy service, we may be used of thee to help one another and to heal the hurt of the world; through the same Jesus Christ our Lord. AMEN.

Passion Sunday

O GOD, who in the death of thy beloved Son didst endure for our sake the agony of the cross; grant to us, we beseech thee, such a measure of thy Spirit that we may not shrink from loss or pain in thy service but may do all we can under thee to help one another and to promote justice and peace upon earth. Forbid that we should complain of burdens and ills that are not worthy to be compared with the sufferings of Christ or the wounds of many among his faithful disciples. Save us from the weakness and futility of self-pity, and from faithless brooding and anxiety. Give us grace to forget ourselves in concern for others. Teach us to find healing for our hurt in unwearied effort to heal the hurt of the world. Fill us with thine own compassion for the sick, the hungry, the lonely, the discouraged, and for all who are victims of prejudice and injustice, that we may enter into the constancy and joy of thy service, and be able to comfort those who are in any affliction with the comfort wherewith we ourselves are comforted of thee; through Jesus Christ our Lord. AMEN.

Palm Sunday

O GOD, whose blessed Son did at this time come in great humility to the city where he was to suffer and die; great is thy goodness and power, who didst not leave him in the grave forsaken but didst raise him up and highly exalt him and give him the name that is above every name. Forbid, O merciful Father, that we in this time should betray the cause of Christ, putting private gain before the welfare of the people and the things that make for peace. Unite us with those who have accepted him as Saviour and Lord and pledged their allegiance to his kingdom. And we beseech thee, give us grace so to follow his teaching and example that we may further his entry into every realm of life, and have a part in his triumph over the forces of darkness and destruction. Hear this our prayer, O thou who art able to keep us from falling and to present us without blemish before the presence of thy glory; and unto thee be glory in the Church and in Christ Jesus throughout all ages, world without end. AMEN.

Good Friday

O GOD, whose beloved Son gave up his life on the cross that we might have life and have it abundantly; we who have known but refused his salvation appeal to thy mercy and seek thy help. Pardon and deliver us, we beseech thee, from tempers and ambitions that make for destruction and death, from all greed of gain, all lust for power, all pride of race or class, all contempt of others, all willingness to reap an advantage at the expense of the poor and the unprotected. Shame and arrest us by the pain of those who have been wounded for our transgressions and bruised for our iniquities. And direct our hearts to the steadfastness of Christ, who consented to suffer at the hands of others but never to inflict suffering upon any man or woman or little child. Give us grace to follow the example of his great devotion, and bring us to his trust and confidence in thee, that so we may be no longer the agents of death but of life and joy and peace; through the same Jesus Christ our Lord. Amen.

Easter Day

Almighty god, who hast brought again from the dead our Lord Jesus Christ and given him the name which is above every name; we rejoice this holy day with unutterable joy in thy great power and glory. By the might of thy Spirit quicken us also, we beseech thee, that we may rise to newness of life, and have a part in the working out of thy purpose of good for the world. Pardon and deliver us from all our sins.

Bestow upon us thy healing and thy peace. And we beseech thee, grant us light upon our way and needed strength for our pilgrimage, until at length by thy great mercy we come to everlasting life.

We pray to thee for those dear to us who have gone before, whom we now name in our hearts before thee. Grant them thy peace, and in thy perfect wisdom and love fulfill thy good purpose for them.

We beseech thee for our brethren in all parts of the world, and most especially for those who are now in sorrow and affliction. O thou who art Father of mercies and God of all comfort, draw near to those in every place who cry for succor, that they may have hope both for this life and for the life to come.

Pour out thy Spirit upon thy Church, that it may do all which may serve and set forward thy blessed kingdom. And we beseech thee, hasten the day when thy holy will shall be done on earth as it is in heaven; through him who for our sake died and was raised, even Jesus Christ our Lord, to whom be glory for ever and ever. Amen.

Pentecost, Commonly Called Whitsunday

O GOD, who at this time didst pour out thy Spirit upon thy Church to abide with it forever; grant that the same Spirit, indwelling our hearts, may keep us from falling; teach us to live according to thy will; enable us for the work thou givest us to do; uphold and comfort us in the hour of trial; beget in us the power to endure faithful to the end; and finally bring us to everlasting life; through Jesus Christ our Lord, who with thee and the same Spirit liveth and reigneth one God, world without end. AMEN.

All Saints' Day

O GOD and Father of mankind, who hast bound together all the generations of men; we rejoice in the communion of thy saints.

We praise and bless thee for all those thy faithful servants whose labor in thee has brought light and hope to the world. For those who were friend to the poor and the weak, defending them against outrage and oppression; for those who went forth as sheep in the midst of wolves to declare thy truth and thy righteousness; for those who, being in thy service reviled and persecuted, did not turn back but continued steadfast to the end; for those who gave up their lives in love to thee and devotion to thy holy cause; for all who in ages past have helped to keep faith and hope and good will alive, we raise to thee our grateful praise.

Give to us thy grace, we beseech thee; that we also may enter into the company of thy saints, and have a part in thy great redemption; and that, with those who have been given the victory over sin and death, we may dwell with thee for ever and ever; through Jesus Christ our Lord. AMEN.

III

Intercessions for Various Subjects and Occasions

Thanksgiving Day

ALMIGHTY and everlasting God, Father of mercies and God of all comfort, we raise to thee our grateful praise.

For the life we have from thee; for the good earth yielding grain and fruits for our sustenance; for the cattle upon a thousand hills; and for the manifold gifts of the sea, we humbly thank thee.

For thy mercies bestowed through the nation to which we belong, and especially for the freedoms won of old by our fathers and cherished and preserved even until now, we humbly thank thee.

For thy prophets and saints whose vision of the Eternal has lighted our path and strengthened our hearts; for valiant souls who, keeping faith and hope in the midst of adversity, shame our doubt and our discouragement; for those near to us and dear who share our joys and our sorrows, and whose love to us never fails; and for all those our brethren whose daily task on land or sea ministers to our good, we praise and bless thy glorious name.

Above all, we thank thee for thyself, O Lord, whose faithfulness is unto all generations. Give us grace, we beseech thee, to show forth thy praise not only in our words but in our lives, by committing ourselves wholly to thy service; through Jesus Christ our Lord. AMEN.

Children's Day

WE PRAISE THEE, O God, for the little children given into our keeping. For their purity of heart, their constant simplicity, their natural and trusting affection, and for the wonderful comfort and joy they bring to us, we praise and bless thy glorious name. Continue, we beseech thee, thy protection to them; and grant to us such a measure of thy Spirit that we may work together with thee for their good.

We remember before thee the many children who are now denied a fair chance in life, all who are hindered by a bad environment, all who are made to toil at an early age, all who are unwanted, neglected, and ill-treated. Make haste, O Lord, for the help of these thy little ones. Suffer us not to add to their burden, or to leave them without a champion for their cause. Fill us with thy holy wrath toward the things whereby they are bruised and afflicted, and by thy great compassion bring us swiftly to their aid. All which we ask in the name of him who took little children in his arms and laid his hands upon them in blessing, thy Son Jesus Christ our Lord. AMEN.

Labor Day

O GOD, whose blessed Son was once carpenter at Nazareth; we pray to thee for the workers of the world. Cheer with thy presence those whose labor is wearisome and joyless, and receive into thy protection those who work in dangerous trades. Look in thy compassion upon all who are exploited or any way ill-treated, and make haste for their help. Give of thy wisdom to all who are in positions of trust, and beget in them a most lively sense of obligation. Rebuke those who through love of money or lust for power would betray their fellows, and in thy great mercy restrain them. Raise up able and unselfish leaders both among those who toil and among those who employ and direct the labor of others; that human industry may be brought under the rule of love, which is the law of life; and that so there may be daily bread for all, and for all the opportunity of growth in mind and heart and soul; through Jesus Christ our Lord. AMEN.

Race Relations Sunday

O GOD, who hast made of one blood all nations of men; give us to know that thou art Father of all, and that we, thy children of every race and nation, are brothers to one another. Suffer us not to close to any the door of fellowship because of their race or color. Make us evermore to remember that whatever we do to one of the least of these our brethren we do to thee, and by thy great love constrain us to seek for all men everywhere the opportunity of fullness of life.

Pour out thy Holy Spirit upon thy Church; that among thy faithful people the lowliest may feel at home, and his heart be warmed, in a fellowship where there is no east or west, no south or north, no bond or free, but Christ is all and in all; and that thy Church, mediating thy love to all sorts and conditions of men, may be for the healing of the nations; through the same Jesus Christ our Lord. AMEN.

The Life of the Nation

ETERNAL GOD, who didst lead our fathers to bring forth in this land a new nation, conceived in liberty; give thy grace to us their children, that we may ever be mindful of thee, without whom no people can prosper or dwell secure.

Pardon, we beseech thee, our sins. We have disobeyed thy holy laws, seeking to enrich and exalt ourselves at the cost of privation and suffering to others. We have consented to bitter want in the midst of possible abundance for all. We have sown discord, division, and strife, and have reaped disaster. O God of our fathers, turn us to thee in hearty repentance and true humility, that thou mayest forgive us our sins and teach us thy will, in which is our peace.

We praise and bless thee for such justice, freedom, and good will as do now exist among us. Give to us the constant aid of thy Holy Spirit, that true democracy may be established in this our land. Uphold us in high resolve that both government and industry shall faithfully serve the people. Enable us to maintain the freedoms won by our fathers. Set us firmly against racial prejudice, and against cruel and humiliating discriminations. Lead us to seek the just distribution of wealth and of the means of education, that all the people may be free to fulfill thy good purpose for them.

O God of the nations, who desirest that all men shall come to fullness of life; give us grace to seek first thy kingdom and righteousness, that thou mayest bless our nation abundantly and make it to be a blessing in the midst of the earth; through Jesus Christ our Lord. AMEN.

World Peace

ETERNAL GOD, in whose will is our peace; we cry unto thee for the ending of war and of preparations for war. Oh make haste, we beseech thee, to save us, lest our cities become heaps and we be left desolate and despairing, going into the holes of the rocks and into the caves of the earth for fear of destruction. In thy mercy turn us from the things that make for discord, division, and strife.

Deliver us from self-righteousness, from foolish pride and boasting, and from all contempt of others.

Deliver us from the desire to impose our will upon others and from consent to reap benefit at others' expense.

Deliver us from putting our trust in bombs and battleships, while neglecting the demands of thy righteousness, the ways of thy mercy, and the adventures of thy faith.

O thou who rulest the world from end to end and from everlasting to everlasting, make us to know that thou art God and that in thee alone is our hope. Grant us grace to repent of our sins and to yield our wills to thine, that thou mayest forgive all our iniquities and heal all our diseases and redeem our lives from destruction. Bring us more and more into fellowship with thyself, O God of peace; that we may have peace within our hearts; and that thou, O Lord, mayest work through us to give peace to the world; through Jesus Christ our Lord. AMEN.

For the Sick

O FATHER of mercies and God of all comfort, be thou present with this thy servant. Grant him thy pardon and thy peace. Enable him to rest in thee. And we beseech thee, give wisdom to those who minister to him in his sickness, and in thy great mercy and power restore him to health, that he may rejoice in thy loving-kindness and devote himself to thy service; through Jesus Christ our Lord. AMEN.

For the Dying

ETERNAL GOD, our heavenly Father, into thy hands we commend the soul of thy servant, in sure expectation of the resurrection to eternal life which thou hast promised; through Jesus Christ our Lord. AMEN.

For the Bereaved

ETERNAL FATHER, who dost share the pain and grief of thy children and art ever ready to comfort those who turn to thee for succor; comfort now, we beseech thee, thy servants who mourn for the loss of one dear to them. Make them to know that those they love but see no longer do still abide in thee, whose years shall have no end, and whose mercy endureth forever. Endue them with strength sufficient for this hour, and grant them thy perpetual grace, that they may continue steadfast to the end, and enter at the last into thy peace; through Jesus Christ our Lord. AMEN.

O MERCIFUL GOD, we cry to thee for the comfort which thou alone canst give. Uphold us in the faith that our beloved, now gone from our sight, is forever secure in thee; and in thy great mercy and power bring us all again together in thy eternal kingdom; through Jesus Christ our Lord. AMEN.

For the Departed

O ETERNAL GOD, who holdest all souls in life; we beseech thee for thy servant ———, whose earthly course is ended. Receive him, we pray thee, into thy eternal kingdom, and fulfill thy good purpose for him. Grant that, increasing in knowledge and love of thee, he may advance in thy service and find therein unending joy and peace; through Jesus Christ our Lord. AMEN.

E TERNAL FATHER, in whose house are many mansions; we pray for our beloved, whose life in the flesh is ended but whose life in thee goes on. Grant him an entrance into the fellowship of thy saints, and of thy tender mercy lead him into thy service more and more, that he may behold thy glory and rejoice in thy peace; through Jesus Christ our Lord. AMEN.

IV

Prayers for the Church of God

ETERNAL GOD, our heavenly Father, who didst come in Jesus Christ to show forth thy love to the world; we praise and bless thee for the Church, through which thou dost continue thy work for us men and for our salvation. We praise thee for a fellowship in Christ that knows no barrier of land or sea but joins together a great multitude, from all nations and kindreds and tongues, in the bonds of a common faith and devotion. We thank thee for the scriptures of thy prophets and saints whereby our minds are instructed in thy holy ways and our hearts are comforted and established in hope. We bless thee for hours of worship when we lift up our eyes and behold, beyond the things that are seen and temporal, the things that are unseen and eternal, and when thou dost draw us unto thyself and give to us that peace which the world cannot give nor take away. Grant us grace to commit ourselves wholly to thee; that we may come to newness of

78

life; and that, belonging to the company of thy faithful servants, we may be used of thee for the extension of thy kingdom upon earth; through Jesus Christ our Lord. AMEN.

WE BESEECH THEE, O God of grace, mercifully to look upon thy Church, that by thy great love and power it may be delivered from evil and may enter into thy service more and more.

Save it from self-righteousness and self-content, and from the easy speech of those who are not doers of the Word but hearers only.

Save it from concern with its own increase rather than with the increase of justice, mercy, and truth.

Save it from love of the glory that is of men, that it may not defer to wealth and power and so betray the welfare of the people.

Save it from pride of race or class, lest it dishonor thee in contempt of thy children and hinder the work of Christ. Oh renew thy people with thy truth and grace, we humbly beseech thee, that thy Church may fulfill its ancient mission: to preach good news to the poor, the sinful, the despairing; to set at liberty

those who are oppressed; and to do all which
may serve and set forward thy blessed kingdom; through Jesus Christ our Lord. AMEN.

O GOD OF PEACE, who didst send thy blessed
Son to preach peace to those who were far
off and to those who were near; we beseech thee
to pour out thy Spirit upon thy Church, that
it may go throughout all the world, preaching
and showing forth in both word and deed the
good news of thy kingdom. Stir up thy people
to make known in every place the ways of
thy laws and the wonders of thy grace; that,
as there is but one God and Father of all, so
there may be one faith, one loyalty and devotion; and that mankind, being united in
thee, may leave the city of Destruction and
move toward the glorious city of God; through
Jesus Christ our Lord. AMEN.

O GOD, who hast given us the commandment
that we love one another even as thou dost
love us; we beseech thee for thy Church
throughout the world. Look in mercy on the
divisions among thy people, and in thy perfect

wisdom teach us to heal them. Take away all blindness of heart, all foolish pride and vainglory, all prejudice, obduracy, and pettiness, and whatsoever else may hinder us from unity in work and prayer for the extension of thy kingdom on earth. Draw us nearer to thee, and firmly unite us in the bonds of a common faith and devotion; that we may all with one voice proclaim thy truth and thy salvation; and that thy Church, being one in thee, may speak a convincing word to a world divided and in awful peril, and so be for the healing of the nations; through Jesus Christ our Lord. AMEN.

ETERNAL FATHER, who hast given the commandment that we should love one another even as thou didst love us in Christ our Lord; give thy grace, we beseech thee, unto us in this parish and congregation of thy people. Teach us to bear one another's burdens, and to show hospitality to strangers. Here may the lonely find a home, and the tempted an house of defense to save him. Here may the heavy-laden find rest unto his soul, and the sorrowing be upheld and comforted. Make us servants of

81

thine infinite compassion, to recover the fallen, to care for the needy, to minister to the sick, and to lead little children into thy holy ways. Draw us unto thyself, O Lord; that we may be united to one another in the bonds of a common faith and devotion; and that, showing forth thy love in both word and deed, we may set forward thy blessed kingdom; through Jesus Christ our Lord. AMEN.

V

After This Manner Pray Ye

Hallowed be thy name

O LORD, heavenly Father, almighty and ever-lasting God, thine is the kingdom and the power and the glory. Thy throne is for ever and ever, and thy faithfulness unto all generations. Thou lookest in compassion upon the children of men; in wisdom and love thou dost draw near to us all and work evermore for our good. Thou didst send thy beloved Son into the world that we might live through him, and hast also given us thy Holy Spirit to guide and help us throughout the whole course of our life.

Oh make us to worship and bow down. Make us to kneel before thee in reverence and humility, confessing our need of thy mercy. Make us to lift up our souls unto thee in adoration and praise, and give us grace to dedicate our lives to thy service.

Let thy name be known throughout all the world. Make manifest among every people thy saving power. Kindle in the hearts of all men the love of justice, mercy, and truth, that thy healing may spring forth speedily and thy blessed kingdom may go forward; through Jesus Christ our Lord. AMEN.

Thy kingdom come

O THOU who art the hope of the world, hasten, we beseech thee, the coming of thy kingdom upon earth. Establish thy rule within us; enter into our minds with thy truth, and dwell in our hearts with thy righteousness and compassion. Establish thy rule in our midst; enter into our homes, our schools and churches, our industry and commerce, all our cities and countries, that the world may be turned from the paths of destruction toward the shining city of God; through Jesus Christ our Lord. AMEN.

Thy will be done

O GOD and Father of our Lord Jesus Christ, Father of mercies and God of all comfort, make us to desire with all our heart that thy holy will shall be done on earth as it is in heaven. Give us grace each day to ask what thou wouldst have us to do; and grant that we may follow thy leading, wherever it may take us, knowing that thou only art wise, thou only art good, thou only art able to lead us in the way ever-lasting, and to save from destruction the things we care for most. O thou in whose will is our peace, bring us into fellowship and co-opera-tion with thee; that we may have peace within our hearts, and that thou, O Lord, mayest work through us to give peace to the world; through Jesus Christ our Lord. AMEN.

Give us this day our daily bread

ETERNAL FATHER, the creator and preserver of all mankind, we gratefully acknowledge our dependence upon thee for all things neces-sary for our sustenance. Thanks be to thee for soil and seed and rain and sunshine, for fruitful trees, for the cattle upon a thousand hills, and for the manifold gifts of the sea. Give us this day our daily bread, that we may be built up in both body and soul, and have strength for the work thou givest us to do.

Forbid, O Lord, that we should ask for more than we need or can rightfully possess. Suffer us not to take from the common store what belongs to our neighbor, or to eat our bread indifferent to our neighbor's need. Keep us ever mindful of those our brothers by whose toil we daily benefit, and fill us with strong desire that they also shall enjoy the fruit of their labor and be built up in body and soul.

O thou who through Jesus Christ didst cause a hungry multitude to be fed, beget in us the same compassion which was in thy blessed Son; that, in a world now able to provide bread for all, none shall go hungry but all shall partake of thy marvelous bounty; and that, in the sharing of bread, we may have blessed fellowship with thee and with one another; through the same Jesus Christ our Lord. AMEN.

*Forgive us our trespasses, as we forgive those
who trespass against us*

ETERNAL FATHER, who art ready to forgive and plenteous in mercy unto all who call upon thee; we thy erring children confess unto thee our sins and beseech thy forgiveness. O God of mercy, be merciful to us who have no hope but in thy mercy. Forgive us all that is past, and grant us the constant aid of thy Spirit, that we may walk henceforth in thy holy ways. Let thy purity cleanse us from all unrighteousness. Let thy compassion make us to abhor cruelty, meanness, and all things whatsoever that are unjust and unkind. In thy vast pity restrain and prevent us from hurting one another and disfiguring our own souls. Let thy great love fortify us against the urgings of lust and the counsels of pride, greed, and selfishness. And suffer us not to nurse feelings of resentment and hate toward those who have injured us. Give us thy grace; that we who stand always in need of thy mercy may ourselves show mercy to others; and that so thou mayest forgive us our sins and bring to us thy healing and thy peace; through Jesus Christ our Lord. AMEN.

Lead us not into temptation

ETERNAL FATHER, who knowest how weak thy children are; lead us not into temptation, but deliver us from evil. It must needs be that temptations come; yet we shrink from conditions that put us to the test, knowing our proneness to sin and folly. O thou who dost not let us be tempted beyond our strength but with the temptation dost also provide the way of escape, save us and help us, we humbly beseech thee.

We praise and bless thee for the working of

thy Spirit within us, whereby we are warned in the hour of temptation, upheld in days of stress, and marvelously comforted amid trouble and sorrow. Give us to know, more and more, that neither life nor death can separate us from thee, and that, whatever as thy servants we may be called upon to do or to endure, thy grace will be sufficient for us.

Draw near, we pray thee, to all who are now sorely tempted and distressed, that, knowing that thou art with them and having daily experience of thy goodness and power, they may fight the good fight, endure to the end, and obtain the victory; through him who ever liveth to make intercession for us, Jesus Christ our Lord. AMEN.

Deliver us from evil

O GOD OF GRACE, who art able to save them to the uttermost who come unto thee; deliver us, we beseech thee, from evil.

From the lust of the flesh and the lust of the eyes, from evil desires and imaginations, from thoughts that torment, weaken, and defile, do thou in mercy deliver us.

From inordinate love of self, from willingness to profit at the expense of others, from taking advantage of the weak and helpless, and from complacence toward evils from which not we ourselves but others suffer, do thou in mercy deliver us.

From worldly standards and false ambitions, from undertakings on which we dare not seek thy blessing, from spending our years for that which is not bread and our labor for that which satisfieth not but is a root of bitterness at the last, O God of mercy, deliver us.

From arrogance and snobbery and all self-righteousness, from harsh judgment upon others with no attempt at understanding and no allowance for human frailty, from all desire to see the guilty not restored but merely punished, and from refusal to forgive those who have sinned against us, O God of mercy, deliver us.

From cowardice before those who have the power to hurt us or to stand in the way of our desire, from putting comfort and security before the demands of thy justice and the working out of thy purpose of good for the world, and from all lack of trust in thy wisdom and power, do thou in mercy deliver us.

O God of grace, show thy mercy upon us, and give to us the constant assistance of thy Holy Spirit, that we may triumph in thy salvation; through Jesus Christ our Lord. AMEN

VI

Litanies

Christmas Eve

I

G LORY TO GOD IN THE HIGHEST.
And on earth peace, good will toward men.

God so loved the world, that he gave his only begotten Son, that whosoever believeth in him should not perish, but have everlasting life.

God, who commanded light to shine out of darkness, hath shined in our hearts, to give the light of the knowledge of his glory in the face of Jesus Christ.

O Lord, holy Father, almighty, everlasting God, who of thy great mercy didst draw near in Jesus Christ to enlighten our darkness, to cleanse us from our sins, and to guide our feet into the way of life;

We praise thee, we bless thee, we worship thee, we glorify thee, we give thanks unto thee for thy great glory. AMEN.

II

REMEMBER Jesus Christ, born that we might

have life and have it abundantly; who lifted
the fallen, healed the sick, was friend to the
poor, the outcast, the neglected, and to little
children; who abhorred cant and cruelty and
all injustice; who, when he was reviled, did
not answer with reviling, and when he suf-
fered, prayed, "Father, forgive them; for they
know not what they do." Thou hast called us,
O Father, to be conformed to the image of
thy blessed Son, even Jesus Christ our Lord.
From unholy desires, from every false ambition, from all pettiness, meanness, and cowardice,

We beseech thee to deliver us.

That we may grow into the likeness of
Christ, sharing his love to every human creature,

We beseech thee to help us.

That we may work for the abolition of poverty and for a just distribution of material
goods,

Grant us the aid of thy Spirit.

That we may set ourselves firmly against
racial discrimination, seeking for all men the
opportunity of a good life,

Grant us the aid of thy Spirit.

That we may labor in all patience and steadfastness to promote peace and good will among men,

Grant us the aid of thy Spirit. Amen.

III

Jesus said: "Fear not, little flock; for it is your Father's good pleasure to give you the kingdom."

For a great multitude which no man could number, out of every nation and kindred and tongue, who through Christ have obtained forgiveness for sin, healing for sorrow, strength for the day, and peace at the last,

We praise and bless thy holy name.

For the forces of good will now at work in the world which flow from the life and death and resurrection of Christ,

We raise to thee our grateful praise.

In the faith that the good work which was begun in Christ can never finally be undone,

We dedicate ourselves this holy night to the end that the kingdoms of this world shall become his kingdom, and he shall reign for ever and ever.

O thou from whom every family in heaven and on earth is named, we commit all who are dear to us to thy love and care.

Grant unto both them and us thy pardon and thy peace, and in thy great mercy bring us all to everlasting life; through Jesus Christ our Lord.

Now unto him who is able to do exceeding abundantly above all that we ask or think, according to the power that worketh in us, unto him be glory in the Church and in Christ Jesus throughout all ages, world without end. AMEN.

New Year's Eve

I

LORD, thou hast been our dwelling place in all generations.

Before the mountains were brought forth, or ever thou hadst formed the earth and the world, even from everlasting to everlasting, thou art God.

Of old hast thou laid the foundation of the earth: and the heavens are the work of thy hands.

They shall perish, but thou shalt endure: yea, all of them shall wax old like a garment; as a vesture shalt thou change them, and they shall be changed.

But thou art the same, and thy years shall have no end.

The children of thy servants shall continue, and their seed shall be established before thee.

O God, whose faithfulness is unto all generations;

Grant that we may in thee abide, now in this time of our mortal life, and in thy eternal kingdom for ever and ever, world without end. AMEN.

II

BLESS THE LORD, O my soul: and all that is within me, bless his holy name.

Bless the Lord, O my soul, and forget not all his benefits: who forgiveth all thine iniquities; who healeth all thy diseases; who redeemeth thy life from destruction; who crowneth thee with lovingkindness and tender mercies.

O merciful God, for thy great goodness in the year which is past,

We humbly thank thee.

Because thou hast not dealt with us after our sins nor rewarded us according to our iniquities,

We humbly thank thee.

Because thy compassions have not failed but thy lovingkindness has been new every morning and thy faithfulness every night,

We humbly thank thee.

For the work we have been enabled to do, for the faith whereby we have been comforted and upheld, for the human love that has warmed our hearts, and for all the simple pleasures that have gladdened our days,

We humbly thank thee.

O thou whose mercy is over all, for the sins we have committed in the year which is past,

Forgive us, we beseech thee.

Thou who willest that we should be pure in heart, from the lust of the flesh and the lust of the eyes, from foolish pride and vainglory, from envy and hate and greed and selfishness,

Cleanse us, we beseech thee.

96

Thou who art our refuge and strength, a very present help in trouble,

Grant that we may fear no evil, knowing that thou art with us.

Thou without whom no sparrow falls to the ground,

Grant that with entire confidence we may entrust all who are dear to us to thy love and care.

Thou who art Father of all,

We beseech thee for our brethren in all parts of the world. Raise up the fallen; relieve the distressed; save the children of the needy; guide the nations into the ways of thy laws; and bring peace to the people.

O God, our help in ages past, our hope for years to come,

We dedicate our lives to thee, and into thy hands we commend our spirits.

Now unto him that is able to guard you from stumbling, and to set you before the presence of his glory without blemish in exceeding joy, to the only God our Saviour, through Jesus Christ our Lord, be glory, majesty, dominion, and power, before all time, and now, and for evermore. AMEN.

The Christian Mission

BLESSED be the God and Father of our Lord Jesus Christ, who out of the great love wherewith he loved us, even when we were dead through our trespasses, made us alive together with Christ, and raised us up with him, and made us sit with him in the heavenly places,

That in the coming ages he might show the immeasurable riches of his grace in kindness toward us in Christ Jesus.

God sent his blessed Son to preach peace to those who were far off and peace to those who were near,

That we all, being reconciled to God through him, might have fellowship with one another.

God caused his Holy Spirit to dwell within us, to bring to our remembrance all that Christ said to us, and to comfort, guide, and empower us,

That we might witness to him in our own community and country, and to the ends of the earth.

98

Go therefore and make disciples of all na
tions, baptizing them into the name of the
Father and of the Son and of the Holy Spirit.

*Thanks be to God for the revelation of his
glory in Jesus Christ, for the indwelling of his
Spirit in our hearts, and for his call to make
known the way of his peace in all places of
the world.*

For the first disciples sent forth by Christ
to heal the sick and to proclaim the kingdom
of God,

We give thee humble thanks.

For the blessed apostle Paul and those who
labored with him to carry the gospel beyond
the borders of Israel, that all the Gentiles
might hear it,

We give thee humble thanks.

For apostolic men who in after years went
throughout Europe, telling of thy marvelous
coming in Christ to bring all men and nations
into thy kingdom, that they might have fullness of life,

We give thee humble thanks.

For all those thy servants who have labored
in this land to bring forth a people instructed
in thy laws and rejoicing in thy salvation,

99

We give thee humble thanks.

For missionaries who in these latter days have gone to Africa, Asia, and the islands of the sea, to publish the good news of thy redemption, and to show forth thy mercy in manifold acts of lovingkindness,

We give thee humble thanks.

For that thy name has been carried to the ends of the earth, and that a great multitude out of all nations and kindreds and tongues have been brought under the influence of Christ and his gospel,

Glory be to thee, O Lord.

We beseech thee for thy missionaries in all parts of the world. Let thy presence comfort them in the hour of loneliness, and thy strength defend them in all dangers and temptations. Give them grace to walk worthily of the calling to which they have been called, forbearing one another in love, serving thee with all patience and all courage, and with humility of mind, that, working through these thy servants, thou mayest lead many out of the darkness of ignorance and sin into the glorious light of thy kingdom.

Amen.

We beseech thee for the young churches established in lands where the gospel is as yet but little known. Give to them thy most wise direction; defend them amid prejudice, misunderstanding, and false accusation; bring them more and more to the knowledge of thy truth and into obedience to thy perfect will, until by thy great love and power they attain to maturity in Christ.

Amen.

We pray to thee for thy Church throughout all the world. Baptize it anew with thy Holy Spirit; that it may kneel before thee in penitence and self-dedication; and that so it may be used of thee to heal the hurt of the nations and to lead mankind into the way of thy peace.

Amen.

O thou who didst give thy blessed Son that the world might have life and have it abundantly,

Help us to give liberally of our substance to thy holy cause, and to give ourselves to thy service.

O thou who art the Lord of the harvest,

Send forth laborers into thy harvest.

O thou in whose hands is the issue of history,

Thy kingdom come, thy will be done on earth as it is in heaven.

O thou whose Spirit helps us in our weakness,

Mercifully assist us in these our prayers, and grant us thy salvation.

Now unto him who is able to do exceeding abundantly above all that we ask or think, according to the power that worketh in us, unto him be glory in the Church and in Christ Jesus throughout all ages, world without end. Amen.

World Peace

O GOD, who art the Father of all, over all and through all and in all;

Have mercy upon us.

O God, who didst give thy blessed Son that we might not perish but have eternal life;

Have mercy upon us.

O God, whose Holy Spirit, indwelling our hearts, would lead us into the way of thy peace;

Have mercy upon us.

Eternal Father, we thine unruly children,

living in a world of disorder and strife in consequence of our many misdoings, pray for thy mercy and seek thy help. From the things in ourselves that make for war,

Save us, we beseech thee.

From pride of race and class, and from contempt of others,

Save us, we beseech thee.

From the desire to impose our will upon others and to exploit them in our own interest,

Save us, we beseech thee.

From consenting to reap benefit at the cost of privation and pain to others,

Save us, we beseech thee.

From delight in power for its own sake and from the use of power for the ends of pride and greed,

Save us, we beseech thee.

From the belief that our nation is a law unto itself and has a right to do whatever it wills,

Save us, we beseech thee.

From false ideas of greatness and glory, and from all cynicism and disbelief in the possibility of a world established in justice and peace,

Save us, we beseech thee.

From reliance on military force rather than on faithful effort to do justly and to promote mutual understanding and trust among nations,

Save us, we beseech thee.

O God, whose rule is over all the world; come among us with great power for our deliverance. Scatter thou the people that delight in war. Put to shame those who call evil good and good evil. Rebuke those whose greed for riches or power is threatening the world with destruction. Raise up in every place men of good will to be thy servants. Multiply them exceedingly, and give to them such a measure of thy Spirit that they may have wisdom, faith, and courage to create the conditions of peace.

Hear our prayer, O Lord, and let our cry come unto thee.

For the promise given of old through thy prophet of a day when nation shall not lift up sword against nation nor learn war any more,

We bless and praise thy glorious name.

For the angels' song at Bethlehem of glory in heaven and peace on earth,

We bless and praise thy glorious name.

For the coming of Christ to be the Saviour of the world and the Prince of Peace; for his teaching and example, his life and death and resurrection; and for the wonder of his rule over the thoughts and lives of increasing numbers of men,

We bless and praise thy glorious name.

That we may know and do the things that make for peace,

Give us thy grace, O God of our salvation.

That we may love our enemies and learn to overcome evil with good,

Give us thy grace, O thou who art kind toward the unthankful and evil.

That we may honor all men and desire and work for the welfare of all,

Give us thy grace, O thou in whose sight every life is dear.

That we may organize the world for peace on the basis of justice and co-operation for the common good,

Give us thy grace, O thou who art the creator and preserver of all mankind.

That we may make disciples of all the nations, teaching them to observe all things whatsoever our Lord Jesus Christ hath commanded us,

Give us thy grace, O thou who desirest all men to be saved and to come to the knowledge of the truth.

That thy Church throughout the world may be one, that Christians everywhere may work together with thee and with one another for the salvation of men and for the healing of the nations, and that so the kingdoms of the world may become the kingdom of our Lord and of his Christ and he may reign for ever and ever,

Give us thy grace, O Lord God, heavenly King, God the Father almighty.

Now unto him who is able to keep us from falling, and to present us faultless before the presence of his glory with exceeding joy, to the only wise God our Saviour, be glory and majesty, dominion and power, both now and forever. AMEN.

INDEX

INDEX

108